my Crystal Journal

my Crystal Journal

A Personal Guide to Healing with 20 Essential Crystals

from bestselling author
JUDY HALL

Krause Publications
An imprint of Penguin Random House LLC
penguinrandomhouse.com

First published in Great Britain in 2022 by Godsfield,
an imprint of Octopus Publishing Group Ltd
Carmelite House
50 Victoria Embankment
London, EC4Y 0DZ
www.octopusbooks.co.uk

Copyright © Octopus Publishing Group Ltd 2022
Text copyright © Judy Hall 2022

ISBN: 978-0-59354-030-5

Printed in China

10 9 8 7 6 5 4 3 2 1

Publisher: Lucy Pessell
Designer: Hannah Coughlin
Editor: Sarah Kennedy
Copy Editor: Clare Churly
Editorial Assistant: Emily Martin
Production Controller: Serena Savini

The information given in this book is not intended to act as a substitute for medical treatment, nor
can it be used for diagnosis. Crystals are powerful and are open to misunderstanding or abuse. If
you are in any doubt about their use, a qualified practitioner should be consulted, especially in the
crystal healing field.

Contents

INTRODUCTION

Long regarded as sacred, therapeutic, and magical items, crystals come in all shapes and sizes and colors. Some have natural facets and points, others are rounded and smooth. Some form clusters, others stand alone. However they look, all crystals are conduits for natural healing energy.

Crystals have been used for millennia to heal and bring balance. They heal holistically—that is to say, they work on the physical, emotional, mental, and spiritual levels of being. They realign subtle energies (see page 14) and dissolve dis-ease (the state that results from physical imbalances, blocked feelings, suppressed emotions, and negative thinking), getting to the root cause.

Each crystal has its own unique qualities that can be harnessed to heal your mind, body, and spirit. So how do we know what each type of crystal does? Well, it's simple. They tell us. The ancients thought that stones were alive but only took a breath every one or two hundred years, and many cultures believed that they were incarnations of the divine. Crystal healers agree that these wonderful gifts from Mother Earth are living beings and see them as incredibly old and wise. Over time healers have gathered an understanding of each crystal's key attributes and functions. For example, Rose Quartz is considered a stone of unconditional love, Aquamarine a stone of courage, and Malachite a stone of transformation.

Journaling and Crystal Healing

This book introduces you to 20 of the most popular crystals and offers 60 ways you can work with them to tackle a wide range of day-to-day issues, from relieving stress and improving your focus to boosting your creativity and tackling emotional issues.

The journal pages have been designed to help you record your experiences working with the crystals. There are prompts to help you get the most out of each healing exercise, but these are only suggestions; use the space to express yourself in whatever way feels beneficial to you.

A journal is a safe space where you can write whatever you think without fear of judgment and without censoring yourself. There is no right or wrong way to journal—you can record everything you are thinking in a stream of consciousness or jot down abbreviated notes about the things you don't want to forget. The only rule you should try to follow is to be as open and honest with yourself as you can.

HOW TO USE THIS BOOK

This book is designed to help you combine the benefits of crystal healing and journaling to improve your well-being. Before You Begin (pages 10–15) shows you how to care for your crystals and introduces you to the methods you'll be using throughout the book. The remainder of the journal presents 20 life-enhancing crystals and shows you how you can tap into their healing powers to enhance your life.

Each crystal entry begins with an introduction to the crystal's attributes and properties, followed by a more in-depth look at three ways you can work with the stone to tackle everyday issues, from lack of confidence to insomnia. Each practical exercise is accompanied by a journal page, including prompts to help you explore your self-development and plenty of room to record your experiences.

This book isn't intended to be worked through in a linear fashion. Instead, flip through the pages until you find a crystal that you are drawn to or see an issue that you would like to explore. There is no rule that you can do an exercise only once; if you find something beneficial you can return to it again. Trust your intuition and go with the flow.

BEFORE YOU BEGIN

Before you dive into the main part of this book, take a little time to read through this section. It will help you understand the best ways to cleanse, activate, and work with your crystals.

Crystal Care

To get the best out of your crystals, you need to know how to cleanse and activate them and how to keep them in tip-top condition.

Sourcing Your Crystals

The best source for your crystals is a local store where you can browse at your leisure. The Internet can point you in the right direction—although there are hundreds of thousands of entries and it can take time and persistence to narrow a search down. There are also Mind-Body-Spirit, healing, and crystal and mineral fairs where you will find crystals for sale.

Cleansing Your Crystals

When you have sourced your crystals, they need to be cleansed and dedicated, as they will almost certainly have lost energy during mining and transportation, and may well have picked up negative vibrations from other potential purchasers. You also need to cleanse a stone after healing, as it will have absorbed energetic toxins.

If your crystal is not soluble, friable, or layered, hold it under running water for a few minutes and then place it in sunlight or moonlight for a few hours to reenergize and recharge it. Delicate crystals can be cleansed in a bowl of raw brown rice, or with sound, light, or a smudge stick. Salt can be used if the crystal is not layered, friable, or delicate. Carnelian cleanses and recharges other crystals if stored with them. You can also buy purpose-made crystal cleansers.

Activating Your Crystals

Once the crystals are cleansed and reenergized, you need to activate them. To activate a crystal, hold it in your hands for a few moments and concentrate on it. Say out loud, "I dedicate this crystal to the highest good of all who come into contact with it." Do this with all your crystals before starting working with them.

Storing Your Crystals

Tumbled stones (ones that have been polished in a large drum with grit, resulting in a smooth and often shiny stone) can be stored together in a bag, but delicate crystals should be wrapped separately and kept in a box when not in use, to avoid scratching them. Adding a Carnelian to your bag or box ensures that your stones are always cleansed and energized, ready for use.

Working With Crystals

Many of the exercises in this book call for you to perform a meditation, ritual, or visualization. Before you begin, find a quiet place where you won't be disturbed, especially by a phone and then sit comfortably and read the text for the exercise all the way through before you start, so you know what to do.

Meditation

Meditating is one of the easiest ways to work with crystals. In the stillness of meditation, the crystals talk to you and you can lose yourself within the crystal. In the peace that follows, solutions and insights rise up into awareness. You don't need to be in a cross-legged yoga pose, just find a comfortable position to sit in for an extended period of time.

Affirmations

Affirmations are simple, positive statements, usually directed toward yourself, that you say aloud with the intention to promote change. Every crystal benefit entry starts with an affirmation. If you don't have the time to try the practical exercise, hold the crystal in your hand, focus your attention upon the stone, and then say the affirmation out loud to help you tune into the crystal's healing energy.

Altars and Vision Boards

Some of the exercises in this book call for you to create an altar or a vision board. Altars need to be situated where they will not be disturbed. You can use a small table, a shelf, a mantel, the corner of a dresser—wherever works for you. Always keep your altar clean and tidy, with fresh flowers and candles as appropriate—and remember, never leave lit candles unattended.

If you make a vision board, you will need to find a place in your home where you can leave it, a place where you can gaze at it regularly and one that won't be disturbed by daily activities. The exercises suggest that you place your crystal on top of the vision board. However, if it is more convenient, and you are using a relatively cheap tumbled stone, you could stick your crystal on top of the vision board and then prop it up to display it instead of laying it flat.

Programming Your Crystal

Some exercises require you to program a crystal with an intention. To program your crystal, hold it in your hands and let yourself be open to higher guidance. When you are totally in tune with the crystal, say out loud, "I program this crystal for [your purpose]." Then put the crystal in a place where you will see it frequently or keep it in your pocket (or a handbag if your clothes don't have a pocket). It can be helpful to hold the programmed crystal two or three times a day, or more. You may need to repeat the programming several times.

Subtle Energy

Many crystal healing techniques interact with the subtle energy of the body and you'll find references to subtle energy and chakras throughout this book. Before your start working with your crystals, you may find it helpful to have a very brief introduction to these concepts.

The Subtle Body

Every living being is surrounded by an invisible but detectable energy field. This subtle biomagnetic sheath that surrounds the physical body provides a protective zone that extends for about 18 inches to 3 ft from the body and contains information about a person's physical, mental, emotional, and spiritual state of being. This traditional name for the human energy field comes from the Greek *avra*, meaning "breeze." The intuitive eye can see dis-ease in the aura.

The subtle energy body around the physical body is made up of six layers: physical, emotional, mental, ancestral, karmic, and spiritual.

The Chakras

A chakra is an energy linkage point between the physical and subtle bodies. The term comes from the Sanskrit word *chakra*, which means "wheel," because these centers appear to clairvoyants and yogis as whirling disks of light. There are seven main chakras, located in a line aligned with the spine:

- Base chakra (at the base of the spine)
- Sacral chakra (below the navel)
- Solar plexus chakra (above the waist)
- Heart chakra (over the heart)
- Throat chakra (throat)
- Third eye chakra (above and between the eyebrows)
- Crown chakra (top of the head)

When the chakras are functioning properly, the body's physical and subtle energies are in balance and harmony. Many energy workers believe that the chakras can be healed by the interaction between the vibrations of crystals and the energies of the body's biomagnetic or subtle energy field.

Amethyst

COLOR
Purple to lavender

APPEARANCE
Transparent, pointed crystals.
May be geode, cluster, or single point.
All sizes

BENEFITS
Making decisions, spiritual
wisdom, sleep

RARITY
One of the most common crystals

SOURCE
United States, Britain, Canada, Brazil, Mexico,
Russia, Sri Lanka, Uruguay, East Africa, Siberia, India

Amethyst is an extremely powerful and protective stone with a high spiritual vibration. It guards against malevolent thoughts and feelings directed toward you, whether consciously or unconsciously, transmuting the energy into love. This crystal's serenity enhances higher states of consciousness and meditation. It has strong healing and cleansing powers, and enhances intuition, spiritual awareness, and psychic gifts.

Traditionally, Amethyst was worn to prevent drunkenness and has a sobering effect on overindulgence and physical passions, supporting sobriety. It overcomes addictions and blockages of all kinds. Used at a higher level, Amethyst opens you to another reality.

Amethyst balances out highs and lows, promoting emotional centering. It dispels anger, rage, fear, and anxiety. Alleviating sadness and grief, it supports coming to terms with loss. It is especially beneficial worn over the throat or heart.

Amethyst &
Making Decisions

*"I am focused and able to make important
decisions when needed."*

Amethyst facilitates the decision-making process, bringing
in common sense and spiritual insights and helping you put
decisions and insights into practice. This stone also helps you feel
less scattered, more focused, and in control of your faculties.
It enhances the assimilation of new ideas and connects cause
with effect.

When faced with a difficult decision, gaze upon a piece of
Amethyst. Focus your mind on the choice you need to make. Ask
the crystal to help you see the potential consequences of each of
your options so that you choose the path most beneficial to you.

When you have finished, use the prompts on the opposite page
to record your experience.

What choice did you need to make?

Which options did the crystal show you?

Which one did you choose?

Why is this the best decision for you?

_____

_____

_____

_____

_____

_____

_____

_____

_____

_____

_____

_____

_____

_____

_____

Amethyst & Spiritual Wisdom

"I am able to connect to the wisdom of the universe in my everyday life."

Amethyst is one of the most spiritual stones, promoting love of the divine and encouraging selflessness and spiritual wisdom. At a subtle level, it balances and connects the physical, mental, and emotional bodies, linking them to the spiritual.

Meditation is a practice used in many spiritual traditions to achieve enlightenment. Amethyst is an excellent stone for meditation because it turns thoughts away from the mundane into tranquility and deeper understanding. When you meditate, try placing an Amethyst on your third eye (above and between the eyebrows) to help you connect to the wisdom of the divine.

In the space opposite, record how it felt when you incorporated Amethyst into your meditation practice, and make a note of any insights your third eye revealed.

The first time I meditated with Amethyst ...

The second time I meditated with Amethyst ...

The third time I meditated with Amethyst ...

_____

_____

_____

_____

_____

_____

_____

_____

_____

_____

_____

_____

_____

_____

_____

_____

Amethyst & Sleep

*"I welcome peaceful dreams and a good
night's sleep."*

Beautiful, calming Amethyst is the ideal crystal to use if you
have sleep problems. It is helpful where insomnia is caused by
an overactive mind and protects against recurrent nightmares.
Placing an Amethyst under your pillow before you go to bed will
help tackle insomnia, fend off bad dreams, and promote restful
sleep. It can help you to remember and understand dreams, and
facilitates the visualization process.

Before you go to bed, place an Amethyst under your pillow
and place this journal and a pen on your nightstand. When you
awake, make a note of the quality of your sleep and any dreams
you remember on the opposite page. Do this for a week and see
whether the quality of your sleep improves.

Aquamarine

COLOR
Green-blue

APPEARANCE
Clear to opaque crystal, often
small and tumbled or faceted

BENEFITS
Calming the mind, tolerance,
finding closure

RARITY
Readily available

SOURCE
United States, Mexico, Russia, Brazil, India,
Ireland, Zimbabwe, Afghanistan, Pakistan

Aquamarine is a stone of courage. It harmonizes its surroundings and protects against pollutants. In ancient times it was believed to counteract the forces of darkness and procure favor from the spirits of light. It was carried by sailors as a talisman against drowning.

Psychologically, Aquamarine has an affinity with sensitive people. It gives support to anyone who is overwhelmed by responsibility. It creates a personality that is upright, persistent, and dynamic. It can break old, self-defeating programs.

Spiritually, Aquamarine sharpens intuition and opens clairvoyance. A wonderful stone for meditation, it invokes high states of consciousness and spiritual awareness and encourages service to humanity.

Aquamarine shields the aura and aligns the chakras, clearing the throat chakra and bringing communication from a higher plane. It also aligns the physical and spiritual bodies.

Aquamarine & Calming the Mind

"I can quiet my mind and my thoughts whenever I want."

Aquamarine calms the mind, removing extraneous thought and reducing stress. It filters information reaching the brain, and clarifies perception, sharpens the intellect, and clears up confusion.

Holding an Aquamarine, say out loud, "I am calm and relaxed right now. I am safe in this moment." Now close your eyes and concentrate on the peaceful feeling of the crystal radiating throughout your body. Notice how the Aquamarine gently clears your mind and helps you feel at peace.

Put the crystal in your pocket or handbag so that you have it with you always. Whenever you feel agitated, briefly hold the crystal in your hand and allow its serene energy to soothe your mind and compose your thoughts.

In the space opposite, record your experience(s) with Aquamarine.

Why did you need to calm your mind?

How did you feel when you used the crystal?

How long did those feelings of calm last?

_____

_____

_____

_____

_____

_____

_____

_____

_____

_____

_____

_____

_____

_____

_____

Aquamarine & Tolerance

*"I accept that everyone is doing the best they can
and I look for the good in others."*

Aquamarine has the power to invoke tolerance of others.
It overcomes judgmentalism and encourages taking
responsibility for oneself. With the help of this crystal,
you can work to become a more tolerant person.

Think of a recent situation when you reacted intolerantly.
Briefly write down what happened on the page opposite.

Now hold an Aquamarine in your hands and ask it to show you
how you could have responded to the person or situation in a
more tolerant manner. Beneath your original description of the
event, rewrite the story, this time using the wisdom of the crystal
to choose a more tolerant response. How did it feel to act more
tolerantly? Remember this feeling next time you feel the instinct
to react intolerantly.

Describe a situation in which you were intolerant.

Rewrite the story, this time choosing a
different response.

Being more tolerant makes me feel ...

_____

_____

_____

_____

_____

_____

_____

_____

_____

_____

_____

_____

_____

_____

_____

_____

_____

Aquamarine &
Finding Closure

*"I choose to let go of the things that are holding
me back. I choose to forgive all others and myself."*

With its ability to bring unfinished business to a conclusion,
Aquamarine is useful for closure on all levels. This stone is helpful
in understanding underlying emotional states, interpreting how
you feel, promoting self-expression, and soothing fears.

Hold an Aquamarine in your hands and connect to the power of
the stone. Meditate on why you need closure. Maybe there is a past
experience or relationship that is holding you back or perhaps
there are things you have left unsaid. Once you have pinpointed
the reason you need closure, ask yourself what it would mean to
accept what has happened and let go of this issue. Think about
the life lessons this issue has taught you, give thanks for those
lessons, then let go and move into the future, unencumbered by
whatever has been holding you back.

On the opposite page, reflect on your need for closure.

Black Obsidian

COLOR
Black

APPEARANCE
Shiny, opaque, glasslike,
all sizes, sometimes tumbled

BENEFITS
Protection, stress relief, acknowledging
your true self

RARITY
Readily available

SOURCE
Mexico and worldwide

Obsidian is a stone without boundaries or limitations. As a result, it works extremely fast and with great power. Its truth-enhancing, reflective qualities are merciless in exposing flaws, weaknesses, and blockages. Nothing can be hidden from Obsidian.

Pointing out how to ameliorate all destructive and disempowering conditions, Obsidian impels us to grow and lends solid support while we do so. This powerful stone can facilitate in going back to past lives to heal festering emotions or trauma that has carried forward into the present. It dissolves emotional blockages and ancient traumas, bringing a depth and clarity to emotions. It also promotes qualities of compassion and strength.

In healing, a Black Obsidian placed on the navel grounds spiritual energy into the body. Held briefly above the third eye it breaks through mental barriers and dissolves mental conditioning. Used with care, it can draw together scattered energy and promote emotional release.

Important: Obsidian is so effective in soaking up negative energies, it is essential to clean the stone under running water each time it has been used in this way.

Black Obsidian
& Protection

*"I am safe and protected from the negative
energies of the world."*

Black Obsidian is a strongly protective stone, forming a shield
against negativity. It provides a grounding cord from the base
chakra to the center of the earth, absorbs negative energies from
the environment, and provides strength in times of need. It also
blocks psychic attack and removes negative spiritual influences.

Hold a piece of Obsidian. Visualize the energy of the crystal in
your hands as a sphere of glowing energy. Imagine that sphere
expanding until it surrounds your body to form a protective shell.
Ask the crystal to hold its protection in place all day.

Carry the stone with you, in a pocket or a handbag, as a reminder
that you are safe and protected. At the end of the day, examine how
you have felt being under Obsidian's protection.

How did it feel to be surrounded by Obsidian's
protective shield?

Did the security it offered you make you act differently?

_____

_____

_____

_____

_____

_____

_____

_____

_____

_____

_____

_____

_____

_____

_____

_____

Black Obsidian
& Stress Relief

"I release all tension from my mind and body."

Black Obsidian is an excellent crystal to draw out mental stress
and tension, and can have a calming effect too. This stone may
bring up the reasons for your stress. When that happens, those
reasons have to be confronted before the problem can be
resolved and peace can return.

Before you go to bed, write any thoughts or worries that are
causing you stress on the page opposite. Sit quietly for a few
moments, holding an Obsidian in your hand, then ask the stone
to draw away your stress while you sleep. Place the crystal by
your bed or under your pillow and put the journal and pen
on your nightstand.

When you wake up, examine how you feel and record
your feelings in the journal.

What were you stressed about before you went to bed?

How did you feel in the morning?

Did the Obsidian bring up any reasons for the stress?

How could you resolve those issues?

_____

_____

_____

_____

_____

_____

_____

_____

_____

_____

_____

_____

_____

_____

_____

_____

_____

Black Obsidian &
Acknowledging Your True Self

"I know who I am and I like who I am."

Black Obsidian helps you to know who you truly are. It brings
you face to face with your true self, taking you deep into your
subconscious mind in the process. This stone brings imbalances
and shadow qualities to the surface for release, highlighting
hidden factors.

Hold a piece of Obsidian. Breathe gently, withdrawing your
attention from the outside world and focus on the crystal in your
hands. Let its energy radiate up your arms and into your heart and
mind. Ask the crystal, "What am I keeping hidden? What riches do
I hold at my core? What am I not recognizing about myself?
Are there any dark aspects to my personality I need to release?"
Take your time and pay attention to all that the crystal reveals.

When you have finished, thank the crystal for the awareness it has
given you, then record your insights on the page opposite.

Blue Lace Agate

COLOR
Pale blue with white or darker lines

APPEARANCE
Banded, often small and tumbled

BENEFITS
Focus, truthful expression,
overcoming fear of judgment

RARITY
Readily available

SOURCE
United States, India, Morocco,
Czech Republic, Brazil, Africa

Blue Lace Agate is a wonderful healing stone. Its soft energy is cooling and calming, bringing peace of mind. It is particularly effective for activating and healing the throat chakra, allowing free expression of thoughts and feelings. It is one of the great nurturing and supportive stones.

Formed from microscopic crystals of Quartz laid down in bands, Blue Lace Agate's multiple layers can bring hidden information to light. It is a very stable and grounding crystal. It has the power to harmonize yin and yang, the positive and negative forces that hold the universe in place. It works slowly but brings great strength.

Psychologically, this stone gently facilitates acceptance of one's self, building self-confidence. Emotionally, it overcomes negativity and bitterness of the heart, healing inner anger, fostering love, and the courage to start again. Spiritually, Blue Lace Agate links into collective consciousness and awareness of the oneness of life. It encourages quiet contemplation and assimilation of life experiences, leading to spiritual growth and inner stability.

Blue Lace Agate & Focus

"Focus comes naturally to me."

Agates can enhance mental function. They improve concentration, perception, and analytical abilities, leading to practical solutions.

Hold a piece of Blue Lace Agate in your hands and connect to the power of the stone—feel its energy radiating throughout your whole being. Gaze at the crystal, carefully examining the bands that surround it. Pay attention to the different shades of blue in the layers of banding. Really concentrate on the tiny details that make this stone unique. Notice how it feels to be this focused on something. Ask the stone to bring you this focus throughout the day.

Carry the stone with you, in a pocket or a handbag. Whenever you find yourself in need of focus, briefly hold the crystal in your hand and allow its gentle energy to focus your thoughts.

When you have finished, use the prompts on the opposite page to record your experience.

How did you feel when you focused on the crystal?

How was your focus today?

What has this crystal taught you about focus?

_____

_____

_____

_____

_____

_____

_____

_____

_____

_____

_____

_____

_____

_____

_____

_____

Blue Lace Agate & Truthful Expression

"It is safe for me to speak my truth."

Blue Lace Agate loves truthfulness. It assists with verbal expression of thoughts and feelings and also clears the throat chakra so that the highest spiritual truths can be expressed.

When you find it difficult to speak your truth, place a Blue Lace Agate on your throat, then close your eyes and ask the crystal to help you see what is stopping you from expressing yourself. If you are uncertain how to express yourself, ask the stone to help you find the right words. If you're afraid of what other people might think, ask the crystal to bring you the confidence to stand in your power and say what needs to be said.

When you have finished, use the prompts on the opposite page to record your experience.

Why do you find it difficult to speak your truth?

What do you want to say?

Who needs to hear these words?

_____

_____

_____

_____

_____

_____

_____

_____

_____

_____

_____

_____

_____

_____

_____

_____

Blue Lace Agate & Overcoming Fear of Judgment

"I allow myself to be who I am without judgment."

Blue Lace Agate counteracts the repression and suppression of feelings that stem from fear of being judged and rejected. Judgment is often present in the parent–child relationship, both in childhood and adulthood. Blue Lace Agate gently dissolves the old pattern of repression and encourages a new mode of expression.

Hold Blue Lace Agate in your hands and feel its supportive energy radiate through your body. Ask the stone to help you reflect on the following questions:

Who do you fear is judging you?

Are you judging yourself?

Are these judgments real or imagined?

What would it be like to live without the need for approval?

How could overcoming fear of judgment change your life?

Write down up to ten things you would do if you had no
fear of criticism or judgment.

_____

_____

_____

_____

_____

_____

_____

_____

_____

_____

_____

_____

_____

_____

_____

_____

_____

Carnelian

COLOR
Red, orange, pink, brown

APPEARANCE
Small, translucent pebble,
often water-worn or tumbled

BENEFITS
Motivation, life purpose,
banishing negative emotions

RARITY
Common

SOURCE
Britain, India, Czech Republic,
Slovakia, Peru, Iceland, Romania

A stabilizing stone with high energy, Carnelian is excellent for restoring vitality and motivation, and for stimulating creativity. At a physical level, it energetically improves the absorption of vitamins and minerals, and ensures a good supply of blood to your organs, muscles, and tissues—necessary for efficient functioning.

Carnelian improves analytic abilities and clarifies perception so that you become more focused. It sharpens concentration, dispels mental lethargy, removes extraneous thoughts in meditation, and tunes daydreamers into everyday reality. With its assistance you can overcome negative conditioning and find steadfastness of purpose.

This stone is a powerful protector against emotional negativity, replacing it with a love of life. Carnelian gives courage, promotes positive life choices, dispels apathy, and grounds and anchors you in the present reality.

Traditionally Carnelian is worn as a pendant, bracelet, or belt buckle. Alternatively, keep it in your pocket to maintain your energy levels. A Carnelian near the front door provides protection and invites abundance into your home.

Carnelian & Motivation

"I have everything I need to succeed."

Filled with vitality, Carnelian is an excellent crystal for energizing any area of your life. This stone restores motivation and gives you the physical and mental energy you need to move forward. If you're a daydreamer rather than a doer, it can help to make things happen.

Hold a Carnelian in your hands and feel its vibrant energy filling you up. Identify one thing you'd really like to achieve today and ask the crystal to help set your intention. Say out loud, "I have the drive and determination to achieve my goal."

Put the crystal in your pocket or handbag so that you have it with you always. If you feel your motivation flagging, briefly hold the crystal in your hand and allow its uplifting energy to give you a boost.

In the space opposite, use the journal prompts to reflect on your experience working with Carnelian.

How did you feel when you held the Carnelian?

Did you achieve what you set out to do today?

Did you stay motivated all day or did your energy
levels fluctuate?

What do you want to achieve tomorrow?

_____

_____

_____

_____

_____

_____

_____

_____

_____

_____

_____

_____

_____

_____

_____

_____

Carnelian & Life Purpose

"I am aligned with my higher purpose."

Carnelian can help you get to the bottom of what makes you tick and give you the courage to trust yourself and make positive life choices.

Holding a Carnelian, breathe gently, withdrawing your attention from the outside world, and focus on the crystal in your hands. Ask yourself what you would like to achieve in life. Then examine whether those things will bring you satisfaction and contentment? If not, ask the crystal to show you things that may be more in line with your life purpose. Be open to whatever the crystal has to show you.

When you have finished, thank the crystal for the awareness it has given you and then write down the insights you received on the page opposite.

Carnelian & Banishing Negative Emotions

"I transform negative energy into love and light."

One of Carnelian's greatest gifts is that of providing powerful protection against negative emotions such as envy, rage, and resentment. If other people's jealousy is blocking your progress, Carnelian releases this. If you have suffered from resentment yourself, this stone calms anger and banishes emotional negativity, replacing it with a love of life that empowers you to manifest your dreams.

Place a Carnelian on a table in front of you and gaze at the stone. Breathe gently, withdrawing your attention from the outside world and into the crystal. Let its energy radiate and embrace you.

Ask the crystal to let you know what negative emotions it would be beneficial for you to release. Notice any thoughts that drift into your mind; recognize if there is a pattern, then let those emotions go with love. Acknowledge any feelings that arise, and lovingly release them.

What negative emotions were you holding on to?

Did you find a pattern in those emotions?

How do you feel now that you have let them
go with love?

_____

_____

_____

_____

_____

_____

_____

_____

_____

_____

_____

_____

_____

_____

_____

Citrine

COLOR
Yellow to yellowish brown or
smoky gray-brown

APPEARANCE
Transparent crystals, all sizes,
often as geode, point, or cluster

BENEFITS
Abundance, self confidence, joy

RARITY
Natural Citrine is comparatively rare;
heat-treated Amethyst is often sold as Citrine

SOURCE
Brazil, Russia, France, Madagascar,
Britain, United States

Citrine is a form of Quartz and therefore amplifies and regenerates energy. Most of the golden-yellow or brownish yellow Citrine sold today is heat-treated Amethyst or Smoky Quartz, which carries the forces of transmutation and inner alchemy. Having been through the fires of transmutation itself, Citrine accompanies you through all the dark places of life and brings you safely out the other side, encouraging you to recognize the gifts in your experience.

This stone promotes enjoyment of new experiences and encourages exploring every possible avenue until you find the best solution. It releases negative traits, fears, and feelings at the deepest of levels. It overcomes fear of responsibility and stops anger. This stone helps you move into the flow of feelings and become emotionally balanced.

Citrine promotes inner calm so that wisdom can emerge. It helps in digesting information, analyzing situations, and steering them in a positive direction. This stone awakens the higher mind and promotes intuition.

Citrine & Abundance

"I receive the abundance of the universe."

Citrine is a generous stone that teaches you how to live abundantly and shows you what true prosperity is. Work with this stone and you will instinctively put out what you most wish to attract in life.

Gather together as many pictures as possible of the things you would like to see in your life—no matter how far out of reach they may seem. Stick the pictures onto a piece of cardboard, overlapping them so that there are no gaps in the energy. When the vision board is complete, lay it down on a surface where you will see it frequently and place a Carnelian in the center (glue it in place if you like).

Once a week, contemplate your vision board. Ask yourself which of the things on your board have manifested in your life—they may not have arrived in the way you expected. Use the page opposite to record your gratitude for the abundance in your life.

I welcome these things into my life ...

Citrine & Self-Confidence

"I can do anything I set my mind to."

Citrine raises self-confidence, enhances individuality, and encourages self-expression. It makes you less sensitive, especially to criticism, and encourages acting on constructive criticism. It helps you develop a positive attitude and to look forward optimistically, going with the flow instead of hanging on to the past.

Place a Citrine over your solar plexus chakra (above the navel). Breathe gently, withdrawing your attention from the outside world and focus on this positive crystal's energy radiating throughout your body, filling you with confidence. Then say aloud, "I program this crystal for self-confidence."

Put the crystal in your pocket or handbag so that you have it with you whenever you need a confidence boost. Carry the Citrine with you for a week and at the end of each day record the small (or large) acts of self-confidence that the crystal supported.

My self-confidence diary:

_____

_____

_____

_____

_____

_____

_____

_____

_____

_____

_____

_____

_____

_____

_____

_____

Citrine & Joy

"Everywhere I go, I attract happiness and joy."

Citrine has the power to impart joy to all who behold it. Its bright yellow color is like a ray of sunshine coming into your life, and can help to lift your mood when you are feeling down. It is the perfect stone to use whenever you wish to stimulate passion or greater joy.

For a week, carry a Citrine with you to surround yourself with the stone's joyful energy. Each evening, spend a little time meditating on your day and then make a list of three things that sparked joy. These things don't have to be huge things, they could be something that made you smile or laugh or something beautiful you heard or saw. Keeping a journal of joyful moments will help you to see the sunny side of life and shift your outlook to a more positive way of thinking.

Write a list of three joyful moments you experienced
each day for a week.

_____

_____

_____

_____

_____

_____

_____

_____

_____

_____

_____

_____

_____

_____

_____

_____

Fluorite

COLOR
Clear, blue, green, purple,
yellow, brown

APPEARANCE
Transparent, cubic, or
octahedral crystals, all sizes

BENEFITS
Learning, opening
the mind, stability

RARITY
Common

SOURCE
United States, Britain, Australia, Germany,
Norway, China, Peru, Mexico, Brazil

Fluorite is a highly protective stone, especially on a psychic level. It helps you to discern when outside influences are at work within yourself and shuts off psychic manipulation and undue mental influence. This stone cleanses, purifies, dispels, and reorganizes anything within the body that is not in perfect order. Used in healing, it draws off negative energies and stress of all kinds and needs cleansing after each application.

Fluorite grounds and integrates spiritual energies. It heightens intuitive powers, makes you more aware of higher spiritual realities, can quicken spiritual awakening, and links to the universal mind. Fluorite brings stability to groups, linking them into a common purpose.

Psychologically, Fluorite dissolves fixed patterns of behavior and gently opens the door to the subconscious, bringing suppressed feelings to the surface for resolution. It increases self-confidence and dexterity, counteracts mental disorders, and is the best crystal to use to overcome any form of disorganization.

Fluorite & Learning

"I absorb wisdom and knowledge."

Fluorite is an excellent learning aid. It organizes and processes information, linking what is already known into what is being learned, and increases concentration. It also helps you to absorb new information and promotes quick thinking.

When you need help studying, hold a piece of Fluorite over your third eye chakra (above and between the eyebrows) and feel the crystal's energy opening your third eye. Stay like this, breathing gently, until you feel calm and undistracted. Say out loud, "My mind is sharp and focused." Now ask the crystal to help you retain information and stay motivated while you work.

Place the Fluorite on your desk while you study so that you notice it whenever you lose concentration. When that happens, remember your intention to study and reset your focus.

In the space opposite, record your experience working with Fluorite.

Fluorite & Opening the Mind

"I open my mind to new ways of understanding the world."

Fluorite helps to move beyond narrow-mindedness, breaking down fixed ideas and helping you to see the bigger picture. It dissolves illusions and reveals truth. This stone is very helpful when you need to act impartially and objectively.

Holding Fluorite, breathe gently, withdrawing your attention from the outside world and focus on the crystal in your hands. Ask the crystal to show you any fixed ideas that are holding you back. For example, is an old-fashioned attitude preventing you from embracing new things or are you finding it difficult to see someone else's point of view. Accept whatever the crystal shows you and ask it to help you examine the issue objectively. Be open to changing your attitude.

When you have finished, thank the crystal for the awareness it has given you, then record your insights on the page opposite.

What fixed idea were you holding on to?

What did you see when you looked at the
issue objectively?

Did this change the way you think?

_____

_____

_____

_____

_____

_____

_____

_____

_____

_____

_____

_____

_____

_____

_____

_____

_____

_____

Fluorite & Stability

"I integrate balance into all aspects of my life."

Fluorite has a stabilizing effect, bringing balance, order, and harmony to mind, body, and spirit. Physically, Fluorite assists balance, coordination, and dexterity. Emotionally, it teaches the importance of balance in relationships. Spiritually, it cleanses and stabilizes the aura.

Hold a piece of Fluorite over your heart. Now close your eyes and concentrate on the peaceful energy of the crystal radiating up to your crown and down to your feet. Feel how your feet connect to the planet beneath you. Feel the stability that the Earth gives you: how it joins with the core of the crystal in a harmonious whole, giving strength to your core being. Before opening your eyes, rest in this feeling of stability for a few moments and ask the crystal how you can introduce more stability into your life.

When you have finished, record your insights on the page opposite.

Garnet

COLOR
Red, pink, green, orange,
yellow, brown, black

APPEARANCE
Transparent or translucent crystal, often
small and faceted or larger opaque piece

BENEFITS
Creativity, regeneration, fortitude

RARITY
Common

SOURCE
Worldwide

Garnet is a powerfully energizing and regenerating stone. It revitalizes, purifies, and balances energy, bringing serenity or passion as appropriate. Garnet is a stone of commitment, inspiring love and devotion, balancing the sex drive, and alleviating emotional disharmony.

Physically, this crystal stimulates the metabolism and regenerates the body. Psychologically, it sharpens your perceptions of yourself and other people. Emotionally, Garnet removes inhibitions and taboos. It opens up the heart and bestows self-confidence.

Garnet is a useful crystal to have in a crisis. It is particularly helpful in situations where there seems to be no way out or where life has fragmented or is traumatic. It fortifies, activates, and strengthens the survival instinct, bringing courage and hope into seemingly hopeless situations. Crisis is turned into challenge under Garnet's influence. It also promotes mutual assistance in times of trouble.

Garnet & Creativity

"I find inspiration everywhere."

Innovative Garnet stimulates light-bulb moments and helps you think outside the box. It motivates you to be more creative in your life and to do the unexpected, empowering your manifesting abilities.

Ask Garnet for help when you want to start a new creative endeavor or are looking for inspiration. Before starting your creative practice, writing, painting, crafting, or whatever else it may be, hold a Garnet in your hands and focus on its energy.

Now set your intention to express yourself creatively. As you inhale, say out loud, "Creativity flows through my body." As you exhale, say, "I release any expectations or judgments about the work I am about to produce." Repeat this several times, until you feel focused and ready to start work. Place the Garnet in a pocket or position it somewhere you can see it while you work.

In the space opposite, make a note of your creative progress.

The first time I was creative with Garnet ...

The second time I was creative with Garnet ...

The third time I was creative with Garnet ...

_____

_____

_____

_____

_____

_____

_____

_____

_____

_____

_____

_____

_____

_____

_____

_____

_____

Garnet & Regeneration

"I release the things that no longer serve me."

Garnet is a stone of regeneration. It is a useful stone for dissolving ingrained behavior patterns that no longer serve you, bypassing resistance or unconscious sabotage, so that you can change and grow. It also removes inhibitions and taboos, facilitating thinking, and doing the previously unthinkable.

To kick-start your metamorphosis, hold a Garnet and breathe gently, withdrawing your attention from the outside world and focus on the crystal in your hands. Ask the stone to help you reflect on the following questions:

What is keeping you stuck?

What do you need to let go of?

What new things do you need to try?

Who do you want to be?

When you have finished, thank the crystal for the
awareness it has given you, then record your insights
in the space below.

_____

_____

_____

_____

_____

_____

_____

_____

_____

_____

_____

_____

_____

_____

_____

_____

_____

_____

Garnet & Fortitude

"I can handle whatever life throws at me."

Garnet offers support during challenges. It is an extremely useful crystal in situations where there seems to be no way out, or where life has become fragmented or traumatic. This stone also promotes mutual assistance in times of trouble, stimulates fortitude and courage, and helps you turn a crisis into an opportunity.

Hold a Garnet over your sacral chakra (below your navel) and ask that it works with you for your highest good. Sit quietly and ask yourself, "What resources do I have?" These resources could be anything or anyone that supports you. They can be external (a friend or family member) or internal (resilience or a talent for problem-solving). Allow the answers to rise up into your mind. Hold nothing back, and give yourself credit for all your positive qualities.

When you have finished, collate a list of all your resources on the page opposite. In times of adversity, use this list to bolster your fortitude.

My external resources are ...

My inner resources are ...

_____

_____

_____

_____

_____

_____

_____

_____

_____

_____

_____

_____

_____

_____

_____

_____

Hematite

COLOR
Silver, red

APPEARANCE
"Brain-like," red or gray when unpolished.
Shiny when polished. Heavy. All sizes

BENEFITS
Strength, resilience,
overcoming compulsions

RARITY
Common

SOURCE
Britain, Italy, Brazil, Sweden,
Canada, Switzerland

Hematite is particularly effective at grounding and protecting. Used during out-of-body journeying, it protects the soul and grounds it back into the body. This crystal harmonizes mind, body, and spirit. It has a strong yang element and balances the meridians, redressing yin imbalances. It dissolves negativity and prevents negative energies from entering the aura, restoring peace and harmony to the body.

Physically, Hematite has a powerful connection with blood. It restores, strengthens, regulates the blood supply, and aids circulation. It can draw heat from the body. Mentally, Hematite stimulates concentration and focus. It enhances memory and original thought. It is a useful stone for the study of mathematics and technical subjects and is said to be beneficial for legal situations. Psychologically, Hematite brings attention to the unfulfilled desires that are driving life, removing self-limitations and aiding expansion.

Hematite & Strength

"My power is unlimited."

Hematite is a strong and grounding stone. It supports timid people, boosts self-esteem and survivability, enhances willpower and reliability, and imparts confidence.

Sit down with your feet flat on the floor and place a piece of Hematite between your feet. Alternatively, lie down and place the Hematite over your base chakra (at the base of the spine). Close your eyes and bring your attention to your base chakra. Visualize a cord of energy extending down from your base chakra and into the Earth—imagine it extending all the way to the center of the Earth, anchoring you to its core. Sense the strength this energy cord offers you and imagine it radiating throughout your body. Ask the Earth to lend you its strength. Once you feel grounded and strong, open your eyes.

Use the journal prompts on the opposite page to reflect on this exercise.

What did it feel like to be connected to the Earth?

What does being strong mean to you?

_____

_____

_____

_____

_____

_____

_____

_____

_____

_____

_____

_____

_____

_____

_____

_____

Hematite & Resilience

*"I see every situation as an opportunity to
learn and grow."*

Hematite helps you come to terms with mistakes and to accept
them as learning experiences rather than disasters. It brings
the mind's attention to basic survival needs and helps to sort out
problems of all kinds.

One of the best ways to build resilience is to understand that
mistakes are inevitable and failure brings growth. Sit quietly
holding a piece of Hematite and connect to the power of the stone.
Think of a recent situation in which you made a mistake. Don't
beat yourself up about the error; instead, reflect on what went
wrong and ask the crystal to show you what you could have done
differently. What lessons can this mistake teach you? What will
you do differently in the future?

When you have finished, thank the crystal for the awareness it has
given you, then record your insights on the page opposite.

Hematite & Overcoming Compulsions

"I have power over my impulses. I resist compulsive urges."

Hematite is a useful stone for overcoming compulsions and addictions. It treats overeating, smoking, and any form of overindulgence. New habits can take a long time to form so repeat the following exercise every day for at least a month, longer if necessary.

Think about a compulsive habit you would like the crystal to help you overcome. Focusing on the Hematite, say out loud, "I program this crystal for overcoming [name the compulsion]." Now close your eyes and sense the strength of this crystal wrapping itself around you. Know that this crystal supports your desire to change. It is willing you to succeed. Carry the crystal with you and hold it whenever you need to be reminded of your intention to break the habit.

Keep track of your progress on the opposite page.

Jade

COLOR
Green, orange, brown, blue, blue-green,
cream, lavender, red, white

APPEARANCE
Translucent (Jadeite) or creamy (Nephrite),
somewhat soapy feel. All sizes

BENEFITS
Self-worth, realizing your
potential, prosperity

RARITY
Most colors are available but some are rare.
Nephrite is more easily obtained than Jadeite

SOURCE
United States, China, Italy, Myanmar,
Russia, Middle East

Jade is a symbol of purity and serenity. Ancient New Zealand lore says that, when given and received with love, Jade takes on the spirit of those who wear it and acts as a link between giver and receiver. Passed down through a family, this stone carries the spirit of the ancestors.

Jade has long used to attract abundance of all kinds. It is believed to attract good luck and friendship. It helps you to be grateful for what you already have and encourages you to become who you really are. It also assists in recognizing yourself as a spiritual being on a human journey and awakens hidden knowledge. Placed on the forehead, Jade brings insightful dreams.

Jade is a protective stone, keeping its wearer from harm and bringing harmony. Jade stabilizes the personality and integrates the mind with the body. It promotes self-sufficiency, releases negative thoughts, and soothes the mind. It also stimulates ideas and makes tasks seem less complex so that they can be acted upon immediately.

Jade & Self-Worth

"All that I seek I can find within me."

A profoundly spiritual stone, Jade helps you see your own self-worth, allowing you to realize that all you need lies within you.

Hold a piece of Jade over your third eye chakra (above and between the eyebrows). Ask this serene crystal to show you who you really are. With its help, accept your thoughts and emotions as they are. With its help, accept your weaknesses and forgive your mistakes. With its help, focus on your strengths and talents. Take a long, hard look at yourself, warts and all. Once you understand everything that lies within you, find a way to love and accept yourself as you are.

When you have finished, take a moment to consider all you have learned and then write a letter to yourself, explaining why you should value your self-worth. In times of self-doubt, reread this letter to bolster your belief in yourself.

Jade & Realizing
Your Potential

"Each day offers me experiences that support my growth and potential."

Jade reminds you to nurture your talents and maximize your potential. Use it to understand how to manifest your best self and to recognize what may have been blocking your efforts. Jade can break down complex ideas so that they become less daunting to put into practice.

Before you go to bed, sit quietly for a few moments, holding a piece of Jade in your hand, then ask the stone to show you how to realize your potential. Place the crystal under your pillow and put the journal and pen on your nightstand.

When you awake, quickly write down the details of any dreams you remember on the opposite page. Holding the crystal, reflect on what those dreams mean. Do they offer any hints about how you can develop and grow?

My dreams were ...

What can your dreams tell you about how to realize
your potential?

_____

_____

_____

_____

_____

_____

_____

_____

_____

_____

_____

_____

_____

_____

_____

_____

Jade & Prosperity

"Success and prosperity are all around me."

Jade is a stone of good fortune. It reminds you that "God helps those who help themselves" and assists you in conserving and making the most of what you have, even when this seems very little. If you have issues around money (whether from lack, over-extravagance, or worshipping this false god), Jade will assist you in overcoming them.

Set up an altar on a shelf or small table. Place your Jade in the center of the altar, then add flowers, candles, and pictures or objects that symbolize prosperity to you. Sit or stand in front of your altar, focusing on the Jade crystal, meditate on what prosperity means to you and invite prosperity into your life.

On the page opposite, write down what prosperity means to you.

Prosperity means ...

_____
_____
_____
_____
_____
_____
_____
_____
_____
_____
_____
_____
_____
_____
_____
_____
_____
_____

Labradorite

COLOR
Grayish to black with blue, yellow

APPEARANCE
All sizes, usually polished: dark until catches light, then iridescent blue or gold flashes. Yellow form is transparent, usually small and tumbled

BENEFITS
Self-belief, insight, transformation

RARITY
Readily available

SOURCE
Italy, Greenland, Finland, Russia, Canada, Scandinavia

Labradorite, also known as Spectrolite, is a highly mystical and protective stone, a bringer of light. It raises consciousness and connects with universal energies. Labradorite deflects unwanted energies from the aura and prevents energy leakage. It forms a barrier to negative energies shed during therapy. It can take you into another world or into other lives. A stone of esoteric knowledge, it facilitates initiation into the mysteries.

This beautiful stone aligns the physical and etheric bodies and accesses spiritual purpose. It raises consciousness and grounds spiritual energies into the physical body. This stone stimulates intuition and psychic gifts, including the art of "right timing," bringing messages from the unconscious mind to the surface and facilitating their understanding.

Labradorite calms an overactive mind and energizes the imagination. It brings up new ideas and balances analysis and rationality with the inner sight. This stone may bring up suppressed memories from the past.

Labradorite & Self-Belief

"I can do anything I set my mind to."

Labradorite banishes fears and insecurities and the psychic debris from previous disappointments. It strengthens faith in the self and trust in the universe.

Hold a piece of Labradorite in your hands and connect with its energy. Ask the stone to help you explore any self-limiting beliefs you may have—the little voice in your head, your inner critic, telling you, "I can't ..." or "I shouldn't ... ," or "I am not ..." and so on.

Gazing at the crystal, challenge each of these beliefs in turn. Recognize the damaging consequences of holding such beliefs. Can you adopt a new, positive belief to take its place? Turn the negative statements into positive ones: "I can ..." or "I should ..." or "I am ... ." Say these new beliefs out loud and feel their truth.

Write a manifesto of self-belief on the page opposite and return to it whenever you doubt yourself.

My manifesto of self-belief:

_____

_____

_____

_____

_____

_____

_____

_____

_____

_____

_____

_____

_____

_____

_____

Labradorite & Insight

*"My mind is strong, open, and clear. I understand
the truth within every situation."*

Labradorite brings contemplation and introspection, synthesizing
intellectual thought with intuitive wisdom. It is an excellent
dispeller of illusions, going to the root of a matter and showing
the real intention behind thoughts and actions.

When faced with an issue that is bothering you, place a piece of
Labradorite over your third eye chakra (above and between the
eyebrows). Feel the crystal's energy opening your third eye. Close
your eyes and meditate on the issue. Ask the crystal to help you
see clearly so that you can understand all sides of the dilemma.

When you have finished, use the prompts on the opposite page
to record your experience.

What was the issue?

What insights did your meditation bring?

How did this change your perspective?

_____

_____

_____

_____

_____

_____

_____

_____

_____

_____

_____

_____

_____

_____

_____

Labradorite & Transformation

"I am courageous enough to change my life."

Labradorite is a useful companion when going through a metamorphosis, imparting strength and perseverance. If you are going through a life-changing event (a new home, relationship, or job, for example) or if you want to change something about yourself, Labradorite can support you on that journey.

Gaze upon a piece of Labradorite. Let your attention be drawn into the shimmering colors of this iridescent stone. When you feel calm and focused, say out loud, "I program this crystal for transformation." Close your eyes and visualize yourself happy, strong, and confident, as who you really want to be.

Put the crystal in your pocket or handbag so that you have it with you always. Whenever you feel the need, hold the crystal in your hand and allow its radiant energy to support you.

Use the prompts on the opposite page to record your experience.

What changes are you going through or seeking
in your life?

How does working with Labradorite make you feel?

What is the next step in your transformation?

_____

_____

_____

_____

_____

_____

_____

_____

_____

_____

_____

_____

_____

_____

_____

_____

Lapis Lazuli

COLOR
Deep blue flecked with gold

APPEARANCE
Dense, veined. Looks like the night sky. All sizes, sometimes tumbled

BENEFITS
Self-knowledge, attunement to the source, self-expression

RARITY
Easily obtained but expensive

SOURCE
Russia, Afghanistan, Chile, Italy, United States, Egypt, Middle East

Lapis Lazuli opens the third eye and balances the throat chakra. It stimulates enlightenment and enhances dream work and psychic abilities, facilitating spiritual journeying and stimulating personal and spiritual power. This stone quickly releases stress, bringing deep peace.

Lapis Lazuli is a protective stone that contacts spirit guardians. It recognizes psychic attack, blocks it, and returns the energy to its source. It teaches the power of the spoken word, and can reverse curses or dis-ease caused by not speaking out in the past.

This stone harmonizes the physical, emotional, mental, and spiritual levels. Imbalances between these levels can result in depression, dis-ease, and lack of purpose. In balance, the harmony brings deep inner self-knowledge.

This stone brings the enduring qualities of honesty, compassion, and uprightness to the personality. It bonds relationships in love and friendship and dissolves martyrdom, cruelty, and suffering.

Lapis Lazuli & Self-Knowledge

"Every day I understand myself better."

Lapis Lazuli encourages taking charge of life. It reveals inner truth and encourages self-awareness.

Hold Lapis Lazuli in your hands and ask that it works with you for your highest good. Think about an area in which you would like to know yourself better and ask the stone to help you understand yourself. For example, you could ask why you fear commitment or need the approval of others. Allow the crystal to help you confront the truth and to accept what it teaches.

When you have finished, thank the crystal for the awareness it has given you, then record your insights on the page opposite.

Lapis Lazuli &
Attunement to the Source

"I am open to the messages the universe has to offer. I accept the truth I receive."

Lapis Lazuli possesses enormous serenity and is the key to spiritual attainment. It encourages creativity through attunement to the Source, connecting you more closely to the divine.

Hold a Lapis Lazuli and breathe gently, withdrawing your attention from the outside world and into the crystal. Let the crystal's energy radiate up your arms and into your heart and mind. Visualize your crown chakra (at the top of your head) opening and imagine a column of pure white light flowing into you. Feel that divine light radiating throughout every cell in your body. Concentrate on this connection with the Source, accepting any impressions it offers. When you feel ready, thank the crystal for helping you and visualize your crown chakra closing. Stay here for as long as you want, then open your eyes.

Record everything you experienced on the opposite page.

Lapis Lazuli &
Self-Expression

*"I am confident expressing my thoughts
and opinions."*

Lapis Lazuli aids in expressing your own opinions without holding
back or compromising. It can also help you to put your feelings
and emotions into words.

Place a Lapis Lazuli on your throat. Close your eyes and think
about a thought, feeling, or emotion you are finding it difficult
to express. Ask the crystal to help you understand why you feel
vulnerable expressing yourself. What do you fear will happen if
you speak truthfully? What is the worst that can happen? Now,
imagine the best possible outcome? Hold on to those positive
thoughts and visualize yourself saying what you need to say.

When you have finished, use the prompts opposite to record your
experience in the journal.

I am scared of expressing myself because ...

This is what I want to say ...

_____

_____

_____

_____

_____

_____

_____

_____

_____

_____

_____

_____

_____

_____

_____

_____

Malachite

COLOR
Green

APPEARANCE
Concentric light and dark bands and rosettes.
All sizes, often tumbled or polished

BENEFITS
Self-acceptance, emotional
healing, spiritual guidance

RARITY
Easily obtained

SOURCE
Romania, Zambia, Democratic Republic
of the Congo, Russia, Middle East

Life is lived more intensely under the influence of this adventurous stone, which encourages risk-taking and change. Malachite amplifies both positive and negative energies. It grounds spiritual energies onto the planet. It is believed by some people that Malachite is still evolving and will become one of the most important healing stones.

This stone mercilessly shows what is blocking your spiritual growth. It brings into the light secrets, deceptions, and sabotage by yourself and others. Malachite draws out deep feelings and psychosomatic causes, breaks unwanted ties and outworn patterns, and teaches how to take responsibility for one's actions, thoughts, and feelings. It releases inhibitions and encourages expressing feelings, alleviates shyness, and supports friendships.

Important: Malachite should be cleansed before and after use by placing it on a Quartz cluster in the sun (do not use salt, which will damage the surface). Always use Malachite in its polished form, and wash your hands after use.

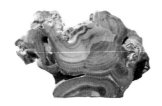

Malachite & Self-Acceptance

"I accept and love myself unconditionally."

Malachite's convoluted whorls help to illuminate all the hidden corners of your mind. It brings to light the inner critic who trips up your best intentions. This stone demands that you take a hard look at all the hidden issues that are holding you back or that are sabotaging you.

Hold Malachite in your hands and connect to the power of the stone. Meditate on why you have difficulty accepting yourself. Ask the stone to show you any toxic thoughts or repressed feelings that are holding you back. Don't be afraid to examine these issues. Let the crystal absorb all the negative energy from these thoughts and feelings, then let them go with love so that you can reclaim your power and move forward.

When you have finished, thank the crystal for the awareness it has given you, then record your insights on the page opposite.

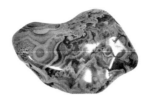

Malachite & Emotional Healing

"I believe in my ability to manifest healing."

Malachite facilitates deep emotional healing, releasing negative experiences and old traumas, bringing suppressed issues to the surface, and restoring the ability to breathe deeply.

Place Malachite on your solar plexus (above the navel) and connect to the power of the stone. Meditate on why you need emotional healing. Ask the crystal to help you identify a past negative experience that is causing you pain. Once you have pinpointed the issue, ask yourself why you are holding on to this pain. What would it take to let it go? Think about any life lessons that negative experience has taught you, give thanks for those lessons, then release the painful memory. Imagine the space it leaves within you filled with unconditional love and move into the future, unencumbered by the pain that was holding you back.

Record your experience on the opposite page.

What negative experience did you need to release?

Why was it holding you back?

How do you feel now that you have let it go with love?

_____

_____

_____

_____

_____

_____

_____

_____

_____

_____

_____

_____

_____

_____

_____

_____

_____

_____

Malachite &
Spiritual Guidance

*"I respectfully ask for Divine guidance in
all areas of my life."*

This stone attunes to spiritual guidance. It can assist in receiving
insights from the subconscious or messages from the future.
Placed on the third eye, Malachite activates visualization and
psychic vision.

Hold Malachite in your hands and connect to the power of the
stone. Gaze at the convoluted patterns of the stone. Visualize
yourself traveling within the stone until you are one with the
crystal. This stone can stimulate pictures in your mind's eye. What
do you see? Pay attention to any images that come into your mind,
without judgment. When you are ready, thank the stone for its
insights, then visualize yourself leaving the stone, until you are sat
gazing at the stone once more.

Use the space below to record the visions Malachite
sent you and reflect on what they mean.

_____

_____

_____

_____

_____

_____

_____

_____

_____

_____

_____

_____

_____

_____

_____

_____

_____

Merlinite

COLOR
Black and white

APPEARANCE
Tendril-like, two-color opaque or translucent
stone, may have an opalescent sheen

BENEFITS
Balance, shamanic journeying,
soul purpose

RARITY
Easily obtained

SOURCE
New Mexico

Merlinite was named after the legendary King Arthur's magician-mentor. This holographic stone holds the combined wisdom of wonder-workers, shamans, alchemists, wizards, magician-priests, and practitioners of magic throughout all ages.

Blending spiritual and earthly vibrations, uniting above and below in a magical correspondence that passes the power of the gods into the Earth, it facilitates access to the spiritual dimensions and to the shamanic realms. It is the perfect stone for magical working because its delicately branching tendrils and flowing layers create pathways that subtly penetrate the veils between the visible and invisible worlds.

Merlinite reprograms ingrained patterns of behavior in the mental and emotional etheric blueprints (imprints of past-life dis-ease, injury, emotional traumas, and mental constructs from which present-life illness or disability can result), bringing about profound change. It assists in coming to terms with negative experiences, turning them into positive learning.

Merlinite & Balance

"I am in harmony with the world around me."

Merlinite's dual coloring brings harmony and equilibrium. It is
the perfect stone for balancing complementary principles such
as the conscious and unconscious or masculine and feminine
energies, and it can help to balance all the chakras.

Hold Merlinite in your hands and connect to the power of the
stone. When your mind feels calm and focused, bring your
attention to your base chakra (at the base of your spine). Notice
how it feels and ask the crystal to gently balance the energy of this
chakra. Then do the same in turn with the other chakras, working
your way up from the sacral chakra (below the navel) to the solar
plexus chakra (above the navel), then the heart chakra, the throat
chakra, the third eye chakra (above and between the eyebrows),
and the crown chakra (at the top of your head). When you have
finished, take a moment to appreciate the harmonious energy
flowing through your body.

Record your chakra-balancing experience on the opposite page.

My base chakra was ...
My sacral chakra was ...
My solar plexus chakra was ...
My heart chakra was ...
My throat chakra was ...
My third eye chakra was ...
My crown chakra was ...

Merlinite &
Shamanic Journeying

"I connect to the wisdom of the universe."

Merlinite helps you to feel secure and protected while traversing the unknown. This stone attracts mentors from other worlds when you first learn the art of magic or shamanism.

To meet a mentor, hold Merlinite to your third eye chakra (above and between the eyebrows) and connect to the power of the stone. Breathe gently in and out. When you feel relaxed, visualize yourself traveling through an ancient forest, following a stream until you reach a secret glade. Take as long as you want to make this journey. Sit down in the forest clearing and ask to meet your mentor. Who (or what) do you see? Greet your mentor and respectfully request that they assist you on future shamanic journeys. Listen to any wisdom your mentor may have to offer. When you are ready, imagine returning through the forest and into your body.

Record your experience on the opposite page.

What did you see on your journey?

Describe your mentor.

Record any insights your mentor shared with you.

_____

_____

_____

_____

_____

_____

_____

_____

_____

_____

_____

_____

_____

_____

_____

_____

_____

Merlinite & Soul Purpose

"All my actions are in harmony with
my soul purpose."

Merlinite helps you to understand your soul's destiny. It assists in reading the Akashic Record (a cosmic record that exists beyond time and space containing information on all that has occurred and all that will occur). Merlinite also helps you to accept that what you think you need may not be what is required for your highest growth and good.

Hold Merlinite in your hands and ask that it works with you for your highest good. Think about a decision you need to make. Ask the stone to show you all possible outcomes. Let the stone show you what might be—your potential futures, depending on the choice you make. Ask Merlinite to help you make the choice that is most aligned with your soul purpose.

Using the prompts on the opposite page, record your experience using Merlinite.

What was the decision you needed to make?

What were the potential outcomes of your choices?

Which choice seemed best aligned with your
soul purpose?

_____

_____

_____

_____

_____

_____

_____

_____

_____

_____

_____

_____

_____

_____

_____

_____

Rose Quartz

COLOR
Pink

APPEARANCE
Usually translucent, may be transparent,
all sizes, sometimes tumbled

BENEFITS
Romantic love, self-love,
heart healing

RARITY
Easily obtained

SOURCE
South Africa, United States, Brazil,
Japan, India, Madagascar

Rose Quartz is the stone of unconditional love and infinite peace. Its empathetic energies help you to love unconditionally and to forgive yourself and other people. This stone of acceptance teaches the essence of true love and instills infinite peace into your heart.

With its powerful emotional healing properties, this stone is excellent during trauma or emotional dramas. It supports you through any challenges and changes in your life, opening you up to manifesting new possibilities.

Rose Quartz is invaluable if you are seeking something to fill a lack. The infusion of unconditional universal love emanating from this stone helps you touch the divine within yourself and fill yourself up from a source that never runs dry. With its assistance, you breathe in love and breathe it out to the world, knowing that there is always more.

Rose Quartz & Romantic Love

"My heart is open to giving and receiving love."

If you want to attract love, look no further than romantic Rose Quartz. When placed by your bed or in the relationship corner of your home (the furthest right corner from your front door), it draws love toward you.

Holding Rose Quartz, say out loud, "I am a magnet for love. I welcome love into my heart and into my life." Now focus on the crystal. Intensely feel what your life is like when you have the unconditional, mutually supportive love of a romantic partner. Send that picture out into the future, unrolling it before you so that you manifest that path.

Place the crystal on your nightstand so that you will be reminded of your desire to manifest love before you go to sleep and when you awake.

In the space opposite, record your experience with Rose Quartz.

What is your life like when you have the unconditional,
mutually supportive love of a romantic partner?

_____

_____

_____

_____

_____

_____

_____

_____

_____

_____

_____

_____

_____

_____

_____

_____

Rose Quartz & Self-Love

"I accept and love myself unconditionally."

Rose Quartz teaches you how to love yourself, and its assistance is vital if you previously thought yourself unlovable. This stone supports the self-acceptance that underlies positive self-worth.

Hold Rose Quartz over your heart and connect to the power of the stone—feel it radiating love throughout your whole being. Ask the crystal to help you recognize why you are worthy of love. Instead of listening to your inner critic, imagine you are your own best friend and describe all your best strengths, qualities, skills, and talents.

Now, using first-person statements, "I am ... ," write down all the reasons to love yourself on the opposite page. Whenever you need to remind yourself of why your deserve to be loved, hold Rose Quartz and read these affirmations of self-love out loud.

My self-love affirmations:

Rose Quartz & Heart Healing

"My heart is free from past hurt. My heart is filled with love."

Rose Quartz is the finest healer. When placed over your heart chakra, Rose Quartz heals emotional wounds and infuses potent loving energies into your heart. If you have never received love, Rose Quartz opens your heart so that you become receptive. If you have loved and lost, it comforts your grief.

Place Rose Quartz over your heart and connect to the power of the stone. Meditate on what needs healing in your heart. Ask the crystal to help release any unexpressed emotions or heartache, transmuting any emotional conditioning that no longer serves, and gently drawing off any negative energy and replacing it with loving vibes.

Using the prompts on the opposite page, record your experience.

What unexpressed emotion or heartache did you
need to release?

How was it holding you back?

How do you feel now that you have let it go with love?

_____

_____

_____

_____

_____

_____

_____

_____

_____

_____

_____

_____

_____

_____

_____

_____

Ruby

COLOR
Red

APPEARANCE
Bright, transparent when polished, opaque when not.
Small faceted crystal or larger cloudy piece

BENEFITS
Courage, passion, letting
go of negative energy

RARITY
Uncut Ruby is readily available,
polished gemstone is expensive

SOURCE
India, Madagascar, Russia, Sri Lanka,
Cambodia, Kenya, Mexico

Ruby is an excellent stone for energy. It overcomes exhaustion and lethargy and imparts potency and vigor to life. This crystal energizes and balances, but may sometimes overstimulate in delicate or irritable people.

Under the influence of Ruby, the mind is sharp with heightened awareness and excellent concentration. It improves motivation and setting of realistic goals. Given this stone's protective effect, it makes you stronger during disputes or controversy.

Ruby stimulates the heart chakra and balances the heart. It encourages "following your bliss." This stone is a powerful shield against psychic attack and vampirism of heart energy. It promotes positive dreams and clear visualization, and stimulates the pineal gland. Ruby is one of the stones of abundance and aids retaining wealth and passion. It is a sociable stone that attracts sexual activity.

Ruby & Courage

"I am bold. I am courageous. I am fearless."

Ruby brings about a positive and courageous state of mind.

Holding a Ruby, say out loud, "I program this crystal for courage." Now close your eyes and concentrate on the fortifying energy of the crystal radiating throughout your body. Notice how the Ruby helps you feel brave and bold, as if nothing were impossible.

Put the crystal in your pocket or handbag so that you have it with you always. Whenever you feel timid or fainthearted, briefly hold the crystal in your hand to remind you how strong and courageous you are.

Carry the Ruby with you for a week and at the end of each day record the small (or large) acts of courage that the crystal supported.

My courage diary:

_____

_____

_____

_____

_____

_____

_____

_____

_____

_____

_____

_____

_____

_____

_____

_____

_____

Ruby & Passion

"I have the passion to take whatever action is necessary."

Emotionally, Ruby is dynamic. It charges up passion, fires the enthusiasm, and encourages passion for life but never in a self-destructive way.

Set up an altar on a shelf or small table. Place your Ruby in the center of the altar, then add flowers, candles, and pictures or objects that symbolize passion to you. Sit or stand in front of your altar, focusing on the crystal. Meditate on whatever passion you would like in your life. Picture it as clearly and intensely as possible. Feel all the joy of having that dream come true. Let yourself really feel what it would be like if this dream came true. Let that power flow into the crystal and ask the crystal to manifest the dream.

In the space opposite, use the journal prompts to reflect on your experience of working with Ruby.

What type of passion do you want to manifest?

What would it be like if this dream came true?

_____

_____

_____

_____

_____

_____

_____

_____

_____

_____

_____

_____

_____

_____

_____

_____

_____

Ruby & Letting Go of Negative Energy

"I acknowledge and release all my negative thoughts and feelings."

Ruby brings up anger or negative energy for transmutation and encourages removal of anything negative from your path.

Hold a Ruby over your heart and connect to the power of the stone. Ask the crystal to show you the negative feelings and emotions you need to release. Maybe you are holding on to resentment or anger or perhaps there is someone you need to forgive. Examine your feelings. What would it mean to let go of these feelings or emotions? Think about the life lessons they have taught you, give thanks for those lessons, then let go and move into the future in love and light.

Use the prompts on the opposite page to reflect on your experience.

What negative thoughts and feelings were you
holding on to?

How were they holding you back?

How do you feel now that you have let them go with love?

_____

_____

_____

_____

_____

_____

_____

_____

_____

_____

_____

_____

_____

_____

_____

_____

_____

_____

_____

Sodalite

COLOR
Blue

APPEARANCE
Mottled dark and light blue-white,
often tumbled. All sizes

BENEFITS
Understanding, self-esteem, intuition

RARITY
Easily obtained

SOURCE
North America, France, Brazil,
Greenland, Russia, Myanmar, Romania

Sodalite stimulates the pineal gland and the third eye and deepens meditation. When in Sodalite-enhanced meditation, the mind can be used to understand the circumstances in which you find yourself. This stone instills a drive for truth and an urge toward idealism, making it possible to remain true to yourself and stand up for your beliefs.

This stone brings about emotional balance and calms panic attacks. It can transform a defensive or oversensitive personality, releasing the core fears, phobias, guilt, and control mechanisms that hold you back from being who you truly are. It is a particularly useful stone for group work, as it brings harmony and solidarity of purpose. Sodalite stimulates trust and companionship between members of the group, encouraging interdependence.

Sodalite clears electromagnetic pollution and can be placed on computers to block their emanations. It is helpful for people who are sensitive to "sick-building syndrome" or to electromagnetic smog (the subtle but detectable electromagnetic field given off by electrical power lines and items such as computers and televisions).

Sodalite & Understanding

"I am open to wisdom, knowledge,
and understanding."

Sodalite is an excellent stone for calming and improving the mind. It eliminates mental confusion and intellectual bondage, and allows new information to be received. It encourages rational thought, objectivity, truth, and intuitive perception, together with the verbalization of feelings. Sodalite stimulates the release of old mental conditioning and rigid mindsets, creating space to put new insights into practice.

Holding Sodalite, say out loud, "I program this crystal for understanding." Now close your eyes and concentrate on the introspective energy of the crystal radiating throughout your body.

Put the crystal in your pocket or handbag so that you have it with you always. Whenever you feel the need for greater understanding, hold the Sodalite in your hand to ask it to help you see beneath the surface of the issue.

Carry the crystal with you for a week and at the end
of each day record how Sodalite helped you achieve
greater understanding.

Sodalite helped me understand ...

_____

_____

_____

_____

_____

_____

_____

_____

_____

_____

_____

_____

_____

_____

_____

Sodalite & Self-Esteem

"I respect myself."

Sodalite enhances self-esteem—the opinion you have of yourself. Sodalite also has the power to bring shadow qualities up to the surface to be accepted without being judged.

One way to boost your sense of self-esteem is to learn to accept compliments. Put Sodalite in your pocket or handbag so that you have it with you always. Next time you spend time with a person you trust, explain that you are working on improving your self-esteem and ask them to give you a compliment. Holding the crystal, listen to what they tell you, without instinctively rebuffing the compliment, and accept the truth in what they say. Say a simple "thank you" for the compliment.

When you have time, write down the compliment on the opposite page. Come back to the page from time to time to read the compliments you have gathered and bask in a renewed sense of self-esteem.

Compliments I have accepted:

_____

_____

_____

_____

_____

_____

_____

_____

_____

_____

_____

_____

_____

_____

_____

_____

Sodalite & Intuition

"My intuition and wisdom guide me in the right direction."

Sodalite unites logic with intuition and opens spiritual perception, bringing information from the higher mind down to the physical level.

Whenever you need to solve a problem, ask Sodalite to activate your intuition and help you make the best decision. Hold the crystal over your third eye chakra (above and between the eyebrows) and connect to its power. Close your eyes and focus your mind on the problem you want to solve. Pay attention to any images that come into your mind or any insights you perceive.

When you have finished, use the page opposite to record the images and insights Sodalite shared with you and reflect on what they mean. Trust your intuition to make the right decision.

What was the problem you wanted to solve?

What did Sodalite show you?

What do you think is the best way to solve
your problem?

_____

_____

_____

_____

_____

_____

_____

_____

_____

_____

_____

_____

_____

_____

_____

_____

Sunstone

COLOR
Yellow, orange, red-brown

APPEARANCE
Clear transparent or opaque crystal with
iridescent reflections, often small, tumbled

BENEFITS
Self-empowerment,
positivity, cutting ties

RARITY
Easily obtained from specialist stores

SOURCE
Canada, United States,
Norway, Greece, India

Sunstone is a joyful, light-inspiring stone. It instills *joie de vivre* and good nature and heightens intuition. If life has lost its sweetness, Sunstone will restore it and help you to nurture yourself. Clearing all the chakras and bringing in light and energy, this stone allows the real self to shine through happily.

Traditionally Sunstone is linked to benevolent gods and to luck and good fortune. This is an alchemical stone that brings about a profound connection to light and the regenerative power of the sun during meditation and in everyday life.

Sunstone acts as an antidepressant and lifts dark moods. It is particularly effective for seasonal affective disorder, lightening the darkness of winter. It detaches from feelings of being discriminated against, disadvantaged, and abandoned. Removing inhibitions and hang-ups, Sunstone reverses feelings of failure and increases self-worth and confidence. If procrastination is holding you back, this crystal will overcome it.

Sunstone is particularly beneficial when used in the sun.

Sunstone &
Self-Empowerment

"I am the author of my own destiny."

Sunstone facilitates self-empowerment, independence, and vitality. Keep this crystal with you at all times if you have difficulty saying "No" and continually make sacrifices for others. Remember, saying "No" to someone else is saying "Yes" to you.

Hold Sunstone over your solar plexus chakra (above the navel) and feel the crystal's vibrant energy radiating through your body. Think about something you really want to do. What is stopping you from doing it? Who or what is holding you back? List all the reasons why you can't do it. Now focus on the Sunstone and imagine saying "Yes." Understand that it is OK to put yourself first. What are the benefits of saying "Yes" to this thing you want to do?

Use the prompts on the opposite page to record your experience working with Sunstone.

What do you want to do?

Why do you think you can't/shouldn't do it?

List all the ways you can say "Yes" to yourself.

_____

_____

_____

_____

_____

_____

_____

_____

_____

_____

_____

_____

_____

_____

_____

_____

_____

_____

Sunstone & Positivity

"I radiate optimism and positivity."

Encouraging optimism, Sunstone switches to a positive take
on events. Even the most incorrigible pessimist responds to
Sunstone. Placed on the solar plexus, Sunstone lifts out heavy
or repressed emotions and transmutes them.

Carry a Sunstone with you all day to surround yourself with its
enthusiastic energy. At the end of the day, spend some
time meditating on everything that has happened and then
make a list of all the positive things you've experienced, no
matter how big or small. Look at the list and appreciate all
the good things life has to offer. Whenever you are feeling sad
or pessimistic, repeat this exercise.

My positive day:

_____

_____

_____

_____

_____

_____

_____

_____

_____

_____

_____

_____

_____

_____

_____

_____

Sunstone & Removing Hooks

"My energy is my own."

"Hooks" are formed when you allow another person to tap into your energy and drain your power. These hooks can be at the mental or emotional level and may come from possessive or demanding parents, children, friends, or lovers. Sunstone is extremely useful for removing hooks, lovingly returning the contact to the other person.

Hold Sunstone in your hands and connect to the power of the stone. Scan your mental and emotional layers and identify any hooks that are draining your energy. When you find one, visualize using the Sunstone's loving healing to gently remove the hook that binds your energy to the other person. Say aloud, "I take back my power. I remove the hook that binds me to [name of person] and let it go with love." Continue to do this until all your emotional hooks have been removed.

When you have finished, record your experience on the page opposite.

What emotional hooks did you find?

How does it feel now you have removed those hooks?

_____

_____

_____

_____

_____

_____

_____

_____

_____

_____

_____

_____

_____

_____

_____

_____

_____

Tiger's Eye

COLOR
Brown-yellow, pink, blue, red

APPEARANCE
Banded, slightly shiny, often
small and tumbled

BENEFITS
Grounding, identifying your needs,
overcoming creative blocks

RARITY
Easily obtained

SOURCE
United States, Mexico, India,
Australia, South Africa

Tiger's Eye combines the earth energy with the energies of the sun to create a high vibrational state that is nevertheless grounded, drawing the spiritual energies to earth. Placed on the third eye, it enhances psychic abilities in earthy people and balances the lower chakras, stimulating the rise of the kundalini energy.

Tiger's Eye integrates the hemispheres of the brain and enhances practical perception. It aids in collecting scattered information to make a coherent whole and is helpful for resolving dilemmas and internal conflicts, especially those brought about by pride and willfulness.

Tiger's Eye is a protective stone that was traditionally carried as a talisman against ill wishing and curses. It shows the correct use of power and brings out integrity. It assists in accomplishing goals, recognizing inner resources, and promoting clarity of intention.

Tiger's Eye & Grounding

"I am calm, safe, and grounded."

Tiger's Eye has a grounding energy that brings about an emotional, physical, and intellectual balance and grounds you in the present. It facilitates manifestation of the will. Placed on the sacral chakra, Tiger's Eye is excellent for people who are spaced out or uncommitted.

Sit with your feet flat on the floor and hold a piece of Tiger's Eye. Breathing gently, close your eyes and visualize roots growing out of the soles of your feet and extending deep into the ground, as if you were a tree. Appreciate how stable and rooted you feel. Imagine using these roots to draw nourishing energy up into your body. Stay here for as long as you want. When you feel calm, collected, and stable, gently bring yourself out of the visualization and open your eyes.

Use the journal prompts on the opposite page to reflect on this exercise.

What did it feel like to be strong and grounded?

How can you carry that energy into your everyday life?

_____

_____

_____

_____

_____

_____

_____

_____

_____

_____

_____

_____

_____

_____

_____

_____

_____

_____

_____

Tiger's Eye & Identifying Your Needs

"I receive all I need from the universe."

Tiger's Eye is useful for recognizing both your needs and those of other people. It differentiates between wishful thinking about what you want and what you really need.

Holding a Tiger's Eye, say out loud, "All that I need comes to me at the right time." Now close your eyes and concentrate on the warming energy of the crystal radiating throughout your body. Ask the crystal to help you meditate on what you need in your life. Ask it to help you see the difference between what you desire and what will serve your highest good.

Use the page opposite to record the things you really need.

A list of my needs:

_____

_____

_____

_____

_____

_____

_____

_____

_____

_____

_____

_____

_____

_____

_____

_____

Tiger's Eye & Overcoming Creative Blocks

"My creativity flows freely."

Fear of failure is a major factor that hinders creativity. Although failure may not seem productive, neither is doing nothing, so don't allow yourself to be caught in the inactivity trap. Tiger's Eye heals issues of blocked creativity. It encourages you to take risks, to do the unexpected, the bizarre, and the surprising.

If you are suffering from creative block, hold a Tiger's Eye and ask it to help you reignite your creative spark. Spend some time letting ideas flow through your mind. Don't censor yourself.

Using the page opposite, write down all the ideas that come to you, no matter how absurd they may seem. No idea is too silly. Keep on writing until you have filled the page. Now, take a look at those ideas and pick one. Don't take too long choosing, just select the first idea that calls to you and do it. Make sure you place the Tiger's Eye in a pocket or position it somewhere you can see it while you work.

Topaz

COLOR
Golden-yellow, brown, blue,
clear, red-pink, green

APPEARANCE
Transparent, pointed crystals, often
small and faceted or large piece

BENEFITS
Manifestation, discovering your
inner resources, problem-solving

RARITY
Easily obtained from specialist stores,
though red-pink is rare

SOURCE
United States, Mexico, India, Australia,
South Africa, Sri Lanka, Pakistan

Topaz is a mellow, empathetic stone that directs energy to where it is needed most. It soothes, heals, stimulates, recharges, remotivates, and aligns the meridians of the body. Excellent for cleaning the aura and for inducing relaxation, Topaz releases tension at any level and can speed up spiritual development where it has been laborious.

Topaz is an excellent emotional support—it stabilizes the emotions and makes you receptive to love from every source. This crystal promotes truth and forgiveness, and cuts through doubt and uncertainty. It brings about a trust in the universe that enables you to "be" rather than to "do."

Negativity does not survive around joyful Topaz. Its vibrant energy brings joy, generosity, abundance, and good health. It has traditionally been known as a stone of love and good fortune, bringing successful attainment of goals. It makes you feel confident and philanthropic, wanting to share your good fortune and spread sunshine all around.

Topaz & Manifestation

"Whatever I desire flows in abundance to me."

Topaz is extremely supportive for affirmations, manifestation, and for visualization. It is said that the facets and ends of a Topaz crystal have both positive and negative energies through which a request to the universe can be focused and then manifested on the earth plane.

Hold Topaz in your hands and ask that it works with you for your highest good. Picture whatever your dream is, as clearly and intensely as possible. Feel all the joy of having that dream come true. Let yourself really feel the power of the dream and how it is when you manifest it in your life. Let that power flow into the crystal in your hand, and ask the crystal to manifest the dream. Put the crystal where you will see it often, or keep it in your pocket to remind you of your dream.

Use the prompts on the opposite page to record your experience.

What dream did you choose to manifest?

What would it feel like if that dream came true?

_____

_____

_____

_____

_____

_____

_____

_____

_____

_____

_____

_____

_____

_____

_____

_____

Topaz & Discovering
Your Inner Resources

"I have complete trust in my inner resources."

Topaz helps you to discover and tap into your own inner resources. This stone promotes openness and honesty, self-realization, self-control, and the urge to develop inner wisdom.

Hold a Topaz in your hands and ask that it works with you for your highest good. Sit quietly and ask yourself, "What inner resources do I have?" Start by thinking about your emotional strengths. Are you patient, compassionate, or empathetic? What else? Now think about your mental abilities? Are you curious, decisive, resilient? Allow the answers to rise up into your mind. Hold nothing back, and give yourself credit for all your positive qualities.

When you have finished, write a list of all your inner resources on the page opposite. Whenever you have a problem to solve, revisit this list to remind you of your hidden strengths.

My inner resources:

_____

_____

_____

_____

_____

_____

_____

_____

_____

_____

_____

_____

_____

_____

_____

Topaz & Problem-Solving

"All the answers I need are within me already."

Topaz aids problem-solving and is particularly useful for those engaged in the arts. This stone has the capacity to see both the bigger picture and the minute detail, recognizing how they interrelate. Once you have solved a problem, Topaz assists in expressing your ideas and confers astuteness.

Before you go to bed, write down a problem you would like to resolve on the page opposite. Sit quietly for a few moments, holding Topaz in your hand, then ask the stone to help you solve the problem while you sleep. Place the crystal by your bed or under your pillow and put the journal and pen on your nightstand.

When you wake up, record the dreams or ideas you had during the night.

What was the problem you wanted to solve?

What did Topaz show you?

What is the answer to the problem?

_____

_____

_____

_____

_____

_____

_____

_____

_____

_____

_____

_____

_____

_____

_____

Picture Acknowledgements

Dreamstime.com Alexandra Barbu 98; Annausova75 86; Anton Novikov 130; Aruna1234 102; Björn Wylezich 104; Bohuslav Jelen 42, 116; Daniel127001 70; Efesan 48; Ekaterina Fribus 30, 68; Epitavi 58, 154; Gozzoli 138; Haotian 94; Henri Koskinen 78; Howard Sandler 64; Infinityphotostudio 66, 122, 124; Jan Fries 22; Jiri Vaclavek 76; Lantapix 20; Martin Novak 62, 128, 144, 148, 150; Mehmet Gokhan Bayhan 110, 118; Michal Baranski 80; Mr.wirachai Moontha 170; Mrreporter 74; Mvorobiev 52; Nastya22 28, 60; Nastya81 114; Olga Frolova 152; Olivermohr 82, 96, 106; Penchan Pumila 88; Phodo 1 164, 160, 166; Photosampler 100; Piksandart 126; Ruslan Minakryn 162; Sergey Lavrentev 50; Vinicius Tupinamba 18, 56; Vladimir Blinov 108; Vvoevale 24, 26, 40, 46, 54, 84, 146, 156, 158; Zelenka68 16, 112

Octopus Publishing Group 32, 34, 36, 38, 44, 72, 90, 92, 120, 132, 134, 136, 140, 142, 168, 172, 174

Unsplash Content Pixie 9; Edz Norton 2; lilartsy 12